Observatory

Andrew Peters

2023
Ingram Spark

Other titles:

Natural Light, 2018
Edge of Light, 2019
Wavelengths, 2020
Lines Written a Few Miles Above, 2023

Orbitals

La Grange Points

Deep Space

Orbitals

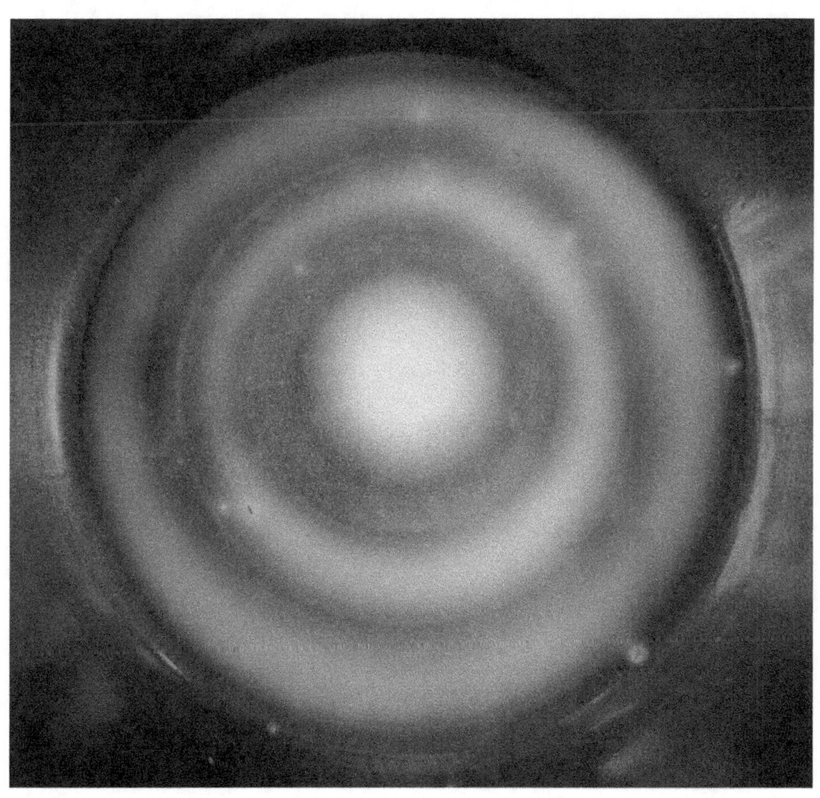

Sandhills

As when the questioning froth of night
flashes the moonlit yearning
of disconsolate years,
the sigh of humble blindness
calms the restless churning
to the settled brew
at the end of the blues
as if the dark in silence
is the end to all the grief
for what will never be.

Like the morning air that breathes
the fearless rising spontaneous
into rustling leaves
pink with gooseflesh song,
the living beat returns
a long sigh alert as if never gone.

The sky spread wide
in thousands of wings glides
the haze of marsh and meadow
seeking places to set down.
In regal splendor red-beaked masks
peruse the avian scene.

With sounds of crane overtures
and wild wings unfurled,
there is consolation in the stride
that wades the grassland green.

And in the stature of sandhill nature
where settles the migrant ritual,
the distant place of turbid dreams
is lost to mists of time
as if unanswerable questions
end in peace.

Birth

At your birth, the greater family
leapt up on legs of gazelles and springboks,
danced with prairie hens and sandhill cranes,
and sang the songs of whales and cicadas.

Your hatchling eyes opened on sights
new to all, unseen by any before,
and your ears newly awakened
heard sounds unheard by any other.

At your birth, you changed all of life
because
such is the way,
new eyes seeing the new
birthed every moment:

the small hand that grips a finger
to lead.

Red Moon

Do not be angry with mystery
peeled from the mute moon
whose choiceless path alters little.
If fullness were the issue,
then perhaps what it ever meant
to be the moon was misunderstood.

All those ages of lunacy,
glorious myths, even longing hopes
never really mattered.

Now with the arrival of the touch,
the giant leap that disillusions,
that only allows simple truth
and unrehearsed beauty,
nothing will ever be the same.

Orbits continue in half darkness.
Reflections appear with equal regularity.

There will always be longing
for one more glorious Dream,
one more grand Imagining,
one more defining Moment
before the full eclipse
and the red moon
yields its lasting message.

Cache

A big cache of thoughts
keeps me going
there jumbled in back corners.

Sure there's the body,
pile of sensations,
pains and pleasures
all this way and that,
but that cache
keeps me going.

Piles of words
and phrases and stories,
snapshots and streams,
and even unreal dreams,
are things I have found,
things that just happen,
pleasant or not,
and things given to me
generously in kindness,
or discarded as useless,
still useful to me.

Now and then I take a few out,
sort them into memories
and ideas for the future,
notions of what should be,
what is, what's gone,
things worth their salt,
things better forgot.

Yes, I admit it is a hoard,
cramming as many as I can
into circadian spaces,
but the trove is so huge by now,
sometimes even nice ones,
treasures even, languish in the dark
until I find them,
often with difficulty,
clean the mild away,
and polish the facets

to a fresh sparkle
and then sort and resort again
into cubes and pyramids and globes.

I try to expunge
those proven wrong
or distasteful, but they
are never totally gone,
always some broken piece
under something
that brings the whole thing back
out of nowhere.

By now these decades past,
I can't find some of the best,
though they have to be here
somewhere maybe sorted
in distracted places.

It's quite a trove
if I do say so,
all treasures really
even the unpleasant gray
and obsidian sorrows.

But you must understand
this glorious beautiful trove
of thoughts
keeps me going,
though I do know,
like everything else,
in the end
I own
            nothing.

Stirrings

The wind always stirs
      up waves
along the surface
    in mysteries of patterns,
phases of interference,

and stirs the sunlit leaves
among the shoreline trees

and stirs wisps of hair
     as if the very air
might misbehave

and stirs memories
     from their deeps
like running with a kite
      until it catches
the wind and tastes
     the sky.

There are reasons behind
     these twists
     and turns,
sciences that would explain,

but like the swirling wind
that comes and comes again,
     turns of the mind
     that result in why
are endless all the same.

Earthfast

I, a creature to movement born,
understand the migrant choice,
the need for rations,
and passions for time.

I, a creature to movement born,
find places that bring great joy,
know the need for nations,
and beauty in every clime.

I, a creature to movement born,
have wondered at all I've been,
the continents explored,
vastness that's gone ignored.

Now as memories rumble
like fading thunder,
I await the foregone wind
whose transience leaves me humble.

I cherish the earthfast trees
who know the value of place
and details we miss in haste.

I cherish the earthfast trees
that allow birds their nests
and provide us shade for rest.

I cherish the earthfast trees
who know of ice and pests
and settle roots to earthen deeps,
holding soil for their solace.

Now this creature to movement born,
seeks out forest keeps
to listen for birdsong words
and whispers in every passing breeze

through leaves.

Oak Trees

Most trees by late autumn have carpeted
the forest floor with dry leaves
already into the work of compost.

But some oaks, especially the red,
though sap has run to ground,
cling to leaves like framed pictures
of children that need an update,
cling through high winds and storms,
as if the clinging were important.

Through the day those leaves
appear crisp and brown,
wrinkled with age and lost energy.

But come morning, clinging leaves
transformed by angled rays
of early sun, shine
with brilliant translucence
of red and gold,
a moment's focus

on hidden radiance
that awaits a change
      of awareness.

Comet

The comet in orbit goes unnoticed
mostly until nearing the sun
the bright tail brings comments.

As passage moves beyond reach,
like a phone call tragic
in the night that steals speech,

perception dulls but for a trace.

As earth traverses the well worn path
it crosses the abandoned course.

Across orbital decades
regular as spinning wheels,
flashes, brief as hope,

like bare-ribbed memories,
appear in the corners of eyes
that never can quite grasp

shattered moments
celebrated until long past
they fade, like visions of solace,

into the vastness of space.

Donut Day

Boxes arrive stacked   thin   unmistakable
in their mystery   of hidden   choices
    that draw   the crowd   down the hall
from offices and cubicles
                    into the break room
      for the grand opening.

Lids lift   to reveal   glazed
delights   plain   old fashioned
    iced   chocolate   maple   strawberry
and there are the cake
        chocolate   blueberry   cinnamon
          and on   special days   twists
    fritters   bear claws   cinnamon rolls
        bags of glazed   and   cake   holes.

There the gathered,
        all political persuasions set aside
rumors ignored   disagreements
    postponed   work left spread
          across waiting desks

all the gathered choose
      a flavor or two
                  pour coffee
and savor   savor   savor
      the moment
          the decadent moment

that carries the day
                  the happy day.

Nesting

Brave wren to consider a nest
left by last year's swallows.
Brave to risk the endeavor
that might be tossed aside
in one brief day.

But who am I to say,
whose thoughts tend toward shallows,
whose unconsidered acts may forever
render all wren-kind
without a viable terrain.

And who am I to speculate
over the wisdom of choices
when I, of the intelligent species,
choose relative ease
over futures for such as these.

So here is the day
and here are the swallows,
who seem to arrive now earlier,
perhaps from heat now on the rise
that shifts their long migration.

And there the brave wren
atop a fence post near,
announcing in a song
clear and strong
unchanged in refrain,
the limits of his domain.

Ah from that song so clear and pure,
his presence feels so sure.

Language of Leaves

Swirling leaves
      block the sun,
and yet patterns
      in negative shades
leave but one
question at the end.

Lost, the forest
allows umbral silences
      that will not fade
when wild winds howl
      the breathless doubt
that would replace
      every name.

Do not mistake
      wild eyes for distrust,
nor fingers clenched tightly
      to this branch or that
for faithless madness.

Rather, there are words
reaching through the cold,
      heard in the heart,
a voice whispering
      the language of leaves

released from branches,
      swirling like pieces
of shattered sky
      to dance with rays
of light.

Feeding Birds

Surely they, wings fluttering as wind
through hair, understand impermanence
better than trees, better than me
who follows day by day routines bent
on fearless comfort.

Surely they know any day now
I may stop and no more
provisioner be,
but in my regularity they return,
independent of my need for the beat
that sustains my heart
making regular my rounds.

My sojourns are proof enough,
for inevitably though unfed
for the duration, upon my return
the first day they are late,
but by the second there they are
knowing I have left seed early,
knowing I am back to patterned habits
in my fleeting days.

So now here they are
doves and finches, cardinals and jays,
titmice and chickadees,
but it's the cardinals with a chit chit,
and chickadees see-deedeedeedee
that look you in the eye

as if they are telling the truth
that assumptions from paradigms
are arguments they quite eschew
for they live without prediction
and perhaps I can do it too.

whistling in the dark

early morning darkness
brings a whistling melody
from some beating chamber,
whistling the dark down,
whistling from some unremembered where,
a random made-up thought
through nautiloid lips

in dim first light the birds join in
with their approval,
or perhaps unimpressed
or with no thought but their way,
opening their cacophony
of messages and declarations
just to start the day

the dog looks at me tilted
as if to say, "and what might be
the meaning of this?"

Behind the Wind

The wind cannot be stopped
rippling the wide surface.
Tips of those waves are unending
seconds awash.

Inevitable passages are fearful
though the sparkling crest is visible.
Though a gentle power
nudges the way,
fear haunts the timeless deeps.

Afraid or unafraid,
adrift or sail hoisted,
intent or unaware,
the wind can not be stopped,
pushing one way to go,
resistance to another.

The tempest, nameless thought,
holds close the swells,
unimaginable in its roar.
Arms of the gale enwrap
the shuddering soul.

Awareness comes in bright sparkles
behind the wind.

Holy in Darkness

They sit on the dock
stooped over, knotting
and reknotting their nets,
intent on the net
and on all those knots,
catching strands,
bringing them together,
managing the tie with the deftness
of human intelligence.

Here and there they test
the strength of it,
pulling strand by strand
the tautness of webbing,
the surety of cords.
Survival depends on the net,
families, communities,
civilizations in need of fish,
silver hope for the future.

Totally in focus, they cast
their nets into water,
leaving patterns on the surface
as the webbing sinks, soon drawn up
again full of the precious feast.

Repairs are always required
as weaknesses are exposed.
They sit on the dock
stooped over, knotting
and reknotting their nets,
intent on nets,
not on the vast darkness
of waters passing through.

Mystics dream of the strand
by strand knotting
connection after connection.
Across the millennia
they build holy places
oriented in the patterns of stars.

At night looking up,
Orion's belt and the great shoulders
must mean something.

Now what was a mystical dream
fades into patterns of light
embedded in the dark surface
imagined.

La Grange Points

Light That Lingers

The light that lingers
has seen it all,
disillusionment of youth,
decline of cities,
extinction of species.
The light that lingers is soft
as the edge of the horizon.

The light that opens eyes has no edge.
Color moves in its warm smile,
hope is its message.
The light that opens eyes is fresh
as unexpected snow,
clear as lifting mists.

The light that burns
ignores inequity,
sees intent in the path,
justice in the swelter.
The light that burns
assumes renewal,
inspires visions for living.

The light that lingers
has seen it all,
passage of moments like drops
on the inevitable surface,
the increasing slant of shadows.
The light that lingers becomes,
in the darkness at the end,
the community of stars.

Incessant

Ours is the incessant mind
that can't stand the jagged edge,
the unfinished look, unmeddled space,
the quiet thought,
brilliant in the morning,
dulled by evening.

Ours is the incessant heart
that can't stand unmanaged dreams,
awkward silence or unwelcome entry,
whose every path must be planned,
every highway an intersect
of culture and intellect.

And yet in every heart there is truth,
in every mind, beauty,
in every nucleic sequence, hope.

I have walked among towering spires
in Chicago like so many others
impressive in metal whelming
and felt cold encircling even the heart,
numbing eyes and ears knowing
just where feet have trod
over neon lights as they reflect.

I have walked among towering spires
of coastal redwoods and heard
in billion needle drift unspoken speech
of warmth encircling even the heart
with a thousand year sigh,
a momentary hush
lingering in the eternal now.

I have waded the coastal shallows
impermanent beneath the wandering
and felt the moving sand awash
in every step through the pull away
to boundless seas and felt the wind
push landward encircling even the heart
with a salty rush

lingering in sparkling curls.

And I have walked ragged paths
among mountain steeps in Colorado,
bare land above the trees,
sat the lakeside reflections
and sat again among hillside rubble
that homes the busy pika,
busy with gathering winter stores,
busy all the brief summer.

Hope

It feels like the last days of summer,
communal ennui adrift in waves
like heat off pavement in the distance.

If it weren't so still as before
tornadic storms maybe there'd be bells,
not bells of awakening, call to worship bells,
but bells before the final silence.

Creatures of the world feel it too.
Sad eyes betray thoughts that cannot be false.

Pervasive heat melts resolves
dripping, into an amorphous pool
like wax around the final flame.

It feels like winter
is an unremembered dream;
red leaves of autumn, a fantasy.

It feels like the end of all seasons,
the whole of earth subsumed
by steaming concrete and asphalt
breathing colors gray and black.

Streaks of neon flash
the heartbeat of ceaseless traffic.

Yet still high in mountains
young elk sing high calls
for mothers and hear replies,

and through tall trees and wild bowers
there is ringing in the paths
of hummingbird wings
believing there will always be flowers.

Eurydice

edges of sky flushed as cheeks
of Eurydice

sunshine through leaves sparkling
as emerald eyes of Eurydice

waves in wide fields golden
as unbraided hair of Eurydice

wind through pine forests whisper
as the sweet sigh of Eurydice

so nature has countless beauties
each with metaphors in Eurydice
countless as drops of rain
pleasures beyond every pain

yet we have set loose the viper,
acrid breath roaming the planet
and here come Stygian floods
overflowing once impervious banks
and here come sweeping fires
as if edges of Stygian plains advance

already too soon she slides
beyond the dreaded veil

would there were perfect rhymes
as in Orphic poems to supplicate

but temples to Apollo are in ruins
mythic stones exposed and broken
and Orphic bargains are known as dreams
forgotten on waking

and so with one last backward look
her imprisonment now is sure
epic poetry at an end

Redwing

For itinerant families
often springtime means a move
friendless to a new place.
Then the summer heat
emphasizes the importance
of family day by day.

In eastern Oklahoma
the summer sun relentlessly sears
lonely hearts and outdoor thoughts
and yet my dad loved to fish.

The tackle box was always full
of artificial flies and lures
but we always started by digging worms
and sometimes shopped for minnow bait
that always saddened the boyish
view of how life should be.

We'd take the canoe for river routes,
but also there were farm ponds,
whose owners my dad somehow knew.

He'd drive the old car down dirt roads,
windows rolled down in the heat,
dust pluming out behind,
until we reached a turnout
and I'd get out
and open the gate in the fence
while he drove through.

Standing there waiting
I could hear them already,
calling from cattails and reeds,
calling as if just to me.

otiro-chee
                    tiro-tweee

We'd carry the gear through tall grass

and when we reached the pond
amidst colors blue and green
there'd be black
managing to grasp
gold rushes
                         otiro-cheee
and then suddenly
they'd fly somewhere beyond
the far side
                         tiro-tweee
and I could see the flash
of red brilliant on their shoulders
in the air.

tiro-tweee
                         otiro-tweee

Dad would bait my hook
until I learned and we'd sit
watching bobbers
in the expanse of silence in between,
waiting for the slightest pull
on tightened lines.

otiro-lee   tiro-tweee

not much was said except about fishing
what next to try,
what kind were stocked,
whether a swallowed hook
might be survived

which allowed time to hear
                         otiro-chee
a grasshopper buzz in flight
a frog jump a sudden splash
                         otiro-tweee
water lap constant on the shore,
persistent breeze a rustle of grass.

otiro-lee otiro-cheee

Most times we'd catch a few perch

sometimes a largemouth bass
special days a catfish,
toss the too small back,
some injured more or less,
but kept the eating size for supper.

otiro-cheee

when the indeterminate time ended
we'd pack the gear
                        otiro-tweee
leaving the line
I inevitably tangled
in trees or bushes
and trace our steps back
to the old car and drive
to wherever we then had home.

I haven't fished in many years
and I doubt I'll go again.
Dad's been gone for decades
and now it doesn't make sense
in the midst of everything else.

But I still remember that flash
of red, the flight of the black,
and I still hear the call
I know will always be there
among rushes and reeds,
calling along the shorelines
as if saying all the things
that have always gone unsaid.

otiro-cheee   otiro-tweee

Farmer

to Wendell Barry

I believe you.
I have seen the earth rise
into your calloused fingers,
past swollen knuckles
and on through your wrinkled hands.

Your words fall to the ground like rain
through ears and through the heart
in search of roots that sustain.
I hear you all right,
your rhyme pitched at first light
as if an end to the dark
is in sight.

I have tasted the bread
of your communion
and found it filling.
I am drunk with the wine
and found I am willing
to spread your message

though mine is a pale bulb of light
when the plowed field
needs the breadth of sun,
the depth of a soaking rain.

I do love the beauty of patterned rows,
and yet a billowing dust rises
before us in the heat,
and I wonder, if I may,
whether the wilder fruit
is not the way.

Hawk's View

Motionless the soaring hawk hangs
in the embrace of wind,
wings tilted at the point
of exact balance.

Imagine such a view:
smallest details of fleeting life
running through distant grasses
and purple mists spread
to the farthest limits of wide skies.

Rooted to earth,
there is no feeling of the soft pull
ruffling feathers,
no knowing the measure
of unchallenged swiftness.

And yet suddenly a moment
sweeps to a breathless
present, balances a delicate
embrace of grass whispering
close by simultaneous
with a distant hiss of mists,

as if perspectives might be entangled
like distant hearts beating,
two particles spinning
an honest moment.

Sometimes Rain Isn't Enough

sometimes rain isn't enough
even sheets running down panes
cascading over gravel streets
making smooth all that is rough

sometimes rain isn't enough
when what could have been
is left a smoldering pile
the results of climate change
they say because they can't say
sometimes rain is not enough

or when you are lost
and can't go back
to start over to find
the rain again to know
where you are
and then you know
that rain is not enough

or with the passage of time
in a long drought
that leaves the earth cracked dry
but never forgets rain
it's just that sometimes
rain is not enough

no sometimes rain isn't enough
good and essential to life
as it is clearing the air,
healing the cracked soil,
washing clean the worn path
wetting down the wild heart
and stiffness from clothes

sometimes a soothing peace
sometimes a great danger

no every drop a memory
sometimes rain is not enough.

39

Flowing

Woods encroach edges of the worn path
where dust adrift forms the center flow
clinging to those who pass by.

And along the river edge reeds
and cattails wave in muddy shallows
pulled by the ceaseless current.

Light transiting millennia
by the millions blur along the edges
but otherwise go unslowed.

For a long time, too long,
I sought to sort tangles beside the path,
while dust that seemed so settled
was always moving in the flow.

I sought to make something
of the immobile shore,
while the placid water surface
disguised the deeper current.

I sought to argue with darkness
about the nature of light,
effects of gravity on mass,
while days were undeniably bright.

Living mostly along edges
listening for music flowing,
seeing dust floating
          water sparkling
          shafts of light flashing,

I thought (as you might)
nothing comes from chaos
                    from stillness
                    from darkness

but there is a peace whispering
through tangled woods
and steadfast shores

and rims of dusk,

and soon, I've come to believe,
somewhere sometime beyond edges
I will be joining
            the everlasting flowing.

Roads Traveled

Often I go as the Poet suggests
choosing this over that path
with no mind for success

Some days are built on nothing
but routine after routine,
others with choice after choice,
banal or at times extreme.

I most enjoy those in between,
especially when in singing voice
moments arise I'm made to laugh,
and dark tones skitter away unseen.

Perhaps each way leads to a different star,
counted uncountably as they are.
They're such a long way and I've not gotten far.

On Being

In the arc of being I lost the way
swayed by shining city streets
and shallow fields of endless play
where time follows an empty beat.

I always planned to return some day
like birds that follow their inner guide
but faster than you or I can say
time runs along a quickening stride.

So here now I've lost all pride,
clever time has stolen it away.
My mind is leaking somewhere inside,
and cold cold joints bring sad dismay.

Yet grace lives in each way of being
and breathless I watch what next to see.

Windsong

There must have been a lullaby
once that softened the cry,
and there must have been refrains
enough sitting with harmonies
running lengths of wooden pews.

Who remembers such things
as days and years pass
unnoticed as the breeze
that shakes the tender grass?

Countless are the songs
that danced so many nights
that some day will reach the stars,
all vibrance let loose
too vast for earth.

They do return again and again,
unfettered unstoppable
through the mind,
orbital memories reverberant
to the heart,
stardust melodies singing
the soul into being
the embodiment of time.

In the end what is left?
Yearning for the lullaby voice,
the four-part hymns,
the heart poured out upon the stage,
the rhythms that drove the dance,
all the echoes fade.

The wind doesn't hear
the silence left behind.

The Other Side

Something there is that loves a wall,
the smell of earth and limestone
rising clear, lifting edges to the sky,

rows of rough-hewn rock standing tall,
the weight of the past holding
the future unreachably high.

something there loves being apart
to calm the rampant heart
and all the vagrant mind demands
whenever chaos comes too close.

Something loves the partitioning art,
clear-cut categories to understand,
and oh echoes resounding echoes

that fade to solitary silence.

<h1 style="text-align:center">Gladness</h1>

I would embrace strong limbs
holding me close to the sky
and look the knotted eyes
in the eye breathing the green
breath of leaves.

I would dream boyhood dreams
of dangers surpassed and fears
vanquished, of kings and queens
and knights with no peers,
lonesome for all the good done,

dreams all clinging to ridged bark
smelling the cool shade,
hearing the rustling dance.

And I would stay the day
in my own private ark,
learning secrets of sap,
smoothness of cambium,
seeing the heartwood and pith
of broken branches

until time for meals
or when the reclining sun
would coax me in.

I was glad for those days
of unmeasured time,
glad for the ways
I learned the rhyme
of wind through limbs
and flickering leaves.

And I am glad still
though climbing is done,
glad for all the between,
springtime flowers of dogwood,
redbud, and apricot,
summer fruit from apples,
pecans and peaches,

autumnal brilliance in red
and yellow, maple and oak,
sweet gum and aspen,
and the careful way
snow lines limbs
and ice hangs from ends,

glad for walks among majesty
in the steadfast shade
of ancient bristlecone,
sequoia and pine trees,
glad for the living
that captures light
and everlasting breeze.

Stars

we don't see things as they are,
we see them as we are -- Anais Nin

a voice says "give up,
there is no emptiness -
the room is not empty,
replete with memories,
the bottle even is still not empty,

and outside, the sky, the sky,
full of stars... "

...and I wonder what are stars?

they could be pin pricks
in the shade of night,
proof of one vast eternal light
beyond the veil of life

they could be the sparkling
surface of a great ocean
or glittering shallows
on dangerous shoals

they could depict mythic stories
of horses and heroes
leading us on,
connecting culture to dream

someone even said once
they are exit wounds,
maybe from shrapnel,
or maybe shattered glass
spread across an asphalt stream

they could be fires
of distant civilizations
awaiting our arrival
or simply focused on their survival

or they could be lights from the great

city on a hill that cannot hide
or perhaps another city in a valley beside
a wandering stream and perhaps each
of us have a home there

perhaps they are souls
lighting the chambers of heaven,
or perhaps they just define
what darkness means,
filling dark matter with light

they could be none or all
of these things
though in fact,

they are infinitely variable,
some unblinking sisters of our earth,
but mostly unreachable suns
of unimaginable magnitude,
and unknowable density,
and some are billions of suns
appearing as a simple one,
all only visible as a distant past

whose meaning dissipates
in red-shifted silence
that is not completely silent,
not completely empty,
just the way we see things.

Deep

Space

Evening Song

Not in the day whose rush
is ever blind would I go;

nor in the senseless night
whose air of finality
is ill suited for leaving.

Perhaps in the morning
amid birdsong hopes
of new beginnings, perhaps.

But sure in the evening slide
        as light lets go,
I will accompany the chorus of frogs
and rustlings of armadillos

into gathering mystery
and the welcoming arms
of darkness.

Entropy

in pieces strewn across the ground
       there it is
the final reward
careless of results

we want to believe
but no amount of glue
will restore what once was new

all the pieces lying there
are just the clue
      we never get
in the moment entropy won

like the youthful day leaving
for adventures unknown
not knowing the fact
      you can never go home

and now there they are each piece
exposed jagged edges ready
      waiting for something

never looking back to winter

Meditation

It all falls away
from the diminished rage
of fire, streams of smoke
drifting up to clear skies
dissolving far away.

It all falls away
in great avalanches
and slow erosions,
impressive fanfares
and unremembered silence,
joyful dances
and horrific explosions,
every entropic way
it all falls away.

It all falls away,
all the brittle leaves
scatter into ground,
all the mountains erode
into plains,
all the rivers flow
into oceans,
all the loudest sounds
        mellow
in the fade.

It all falls away
nothing left to evoke
the quickened beat,
the hurried step
to some impassioned play.

It all falls away
all the money made,
all the work done,
all the treasures found,
all the power evaporated.

It all falls away,

every gyre unspun,
every edge filed smooth
every wall undone,
every barrier passed through,
every mask removed,
what was hidden, opened,
what was known becomes unknown.

It all falls away leaving
only the unimaginable ground,
vast hallowed permanence
pulling together all the frames,
an unbroken field
of seamless points untipped,
all values resolved
to equilibrium.

It all falls away leaving
only the great symphony
that is all songs
tuned to a single tone,
only the great poem
that is all poems rhymed
to wordless thought
yearning for simultaneous
darkness and light,
where vector and scalar
are the same.

It all falls away leaving
only the grace
that has no place,
only the beauty
in the vast beatitude,
the timeless moment
of gratitude.

It all falls away,
things that were done,
lives left unled,
all the things spoken,
all the thoughts left unsaid.
It all falls away.

let it fall
let it fall
let it all fall
to ground

1

the day ran headlong, brow glistening,
never more in search, the cyclops sun
staring with tense intensity

the memory of it is like feet
leaving misshapen prints in wet sand

it was all a Janis Joplin time,
Bobbie Magee with nothin' left
thinking it all mattered,
                oh but it didn't.

2

the night danced, long hair swaying,
never more in love, stars arrayed
like countless sparkling eyes watching

the memory of it is like bats flitting
around a yard light chasing mayflies

it was all an Otis Redding time,
sittin' on the dock thinking
nothing mattered,
                oh but it did.

3

now the marbled memories
rattle around in a jar,
each a world of its own,
cat's eyes in blue-green,
solid red-yellow swirls,
clear with bubbles afloat,

collected for what?
to pass along?
how can you possibly know
the same moment

that will never be again
but by slanted rhyme?

but, my friend, do not assume
memories to be lost.
there are creatures today
who carry the DNA
of ancestors who swam
the shallow seas before life
had moved upon the land,

and there are birds today
carrying memories of extinctions
embedded in their genes,
so who's to say
but that beings who wrap energy
and matter into spirals of time
send waves of memories off
like the flash of every moment
that even now rides the quantum wave
galaxy to galaxy

and just as every day
there are faded memories
that reappear in vivid relief,
who's to say
that all memories
will one day live afresh.

that night music faded
like childhood voices
from abandoned playgrounds
brass and woodwinds drifted home
vibrance of drums absorbed by silence

     spotlights fading out
the field finally empty spread wider
     joining darkness
     emptying
the quiescent mind

that night leaning against the car
     unaware of any observers
field stretched beyond the darkened sky
     city lights extinguished
darkness closed in
     blinding the future
until the appearance of stars
like pin holes in the quantum shade

passion bloomed that night
streaming from the pulse
     of the brightest star
entangling tears of joy and sorrow
     aches of body and soul
entangling observer and observed

entangling breath of life
     and passing moment
timeless dream and careless thought

photons and waves beyond the shade
suddenly visible in streaming pathways
suddenly that night at a crossroads
of all the endless shining points
     at a moment's choice

that night passion dreamed of joining
the path of that brightest stream
     make of it the guiding way

but then came dawn of the next day
        like the dawn of every day
and the sun like the turning mind
burned distinctions of every kind
        and the path of a lifetime
like the briefness of colored leaves
in autumn drifting to earth
        was lost in the blaze
            of fleeting comforts
            and exigent litanies

yet still the entangled heart
            yearns to dream
still entangled in the night
entangled in the moment believing
despite a lifelong grieving
            the unchosen
that all paths are one
            beyond
the moving shade

whether tumbling cascades
or roaring falls or placid deeps
where eddies spiral among
reedy edges, the current is strong,
its passage a one way song

here and there beauty
in the cast of light
off sharp edges lifts
the startled heart
like a heron in sudden flight

here and there shade
sinks deeply in peace
set adrift
between beats
as if the heart might forget
what has been cast
in animated spray

but even where transit
is difficult raging with panic,
or silent in grieving,
or unsure in darkened frame
of polluted oil-slick film,
beauty swirls a rainbow promise
recollected as a tranquil gift
by the heart calmed as mists
rising off the hazy surface

close to the wide sea
where the stream meets
the open ended horizon
where senses are lost
and passions abandoned,
the heart, the faithful heart
never stops the steady beat
but always follows,

yes that heart, faithful heart
does not forget

the fervored touch of dreams,

yes, that heart, faithful heart,
that beats and beats
for the beauty of tomorrow,
seeking whatever might repeat
or even headlong rhyme,
that heart, faithful heart
does not forget, never forgets
the grateful, intimate sorrow
for all that can never again be.

Unquiet Heart

When night comes along the shore,
waves grow strong, gradual as the song
of the turning moon that says nothing
of darkness, but lifts higher curves
to do their work.

Waves grow strong enough to smooth
the careless sands of their mistakes,
burying flotsam memories
that may have drifted for years but now
find comfort beneath the glistening surface.

Unlike the quiet of forest glooms,
when night comes along the shore
silence gives way to unhushed moans,
as if the very deeps are urged to words
that repeat all the sorrows foregone.

Continuum

at 70 mph blink
and you might miss it
grocery stop at the roadside
where locals drink coffee
and eat fresh donuts
or have bacon and eggs
how you like 'em

where strangers stop
for gas and are on their way
to some important appointment
somewhere or some unwinding
spell cast in beauty elsewhere

time is a place I knew once
where I made my own roads
in sand and mountains of dirt
where I could run with the wind
on youthful knees effortlessly
staying ahead looking back

where in a new house
the room at the end of a long hall
frightened then became refuge
for solitude and mourning doves
roused each new day
of climbing oak tree rustlings

a place where sleeping in a low tent
campfire eggs on a cold morning
and unfettered days in a forest
became the foundation
for timeless tolerance

time is a place I knew
where heritage breathed
a community gathered
in ritual and harmony
that meant belief
even when there wasn't
knowing what to believe

a place where notes I played
in the language of brass
were all the belief
all the words that needed
to be said

time is a place I knew
where there were reasons to slide
off the road in reckless abandon
and figure an unpanicked way
of getting unstuck

a place I knew
where a crackling fire
was forever singing
Eleanor Rigby in the dark
driving home
where I knew just knew
the dance would go on
like bats circling light poles

time is a place I knew
where hospitals couldn't be helped
any more than death
and whether 20 or 60 years
it wasn't enough
a place I knew
where hopes and visions
rose and fell like waves
along the shore
erasing footsteps

a place where a hand
a nearby hand offered
the grip of someplace to go
something to do
someone deathless to know
pulling along along
like the ring that becomes
concentric circles unbroken

time is a place I knew

where rest meant fallen sails
and irresistible currents
written by children
rewriting the story I knew
into shining eyes
and ceaseless play
and some unknowable day

time is a place I know where roads
through mountains shrouded
in mist and wild sounds
wind up and down
hairpin curves
where at even 30 mph or less
you might miss it all
a glade filled with columbines
and blue flax a steep precipice
with yellow stone crop
and pine trees living
through the rocks
on the vertical face

blink and you might miss
the panoramic insight
the knowledge of clear air
you might miss a rock close by
that mimics a mountain top
touching the sky in the distance
you might miss
the roadside cafe
with generous portions
and smiling faces

at speed you might miss it
you might miss it all

Overthinking

In the ice storm the trees bend low
until weakness pops
and the poor branches lie broken
the pleasure of their shade spent

I wonder about the birds
glad for open spaces
or frantic for shelter
frustrated from the decrease
in nesting sites

I wonder about the shortened lives
of trees that had lived a century
and more and about those that could
have seen the next century
but now have a decade or less

I wonder about the understory
shade dwelling plants soon to be
overtaken by sun worshipers
now free to spread
until of course the canopy returns
and the sun lovers go their way

I guess I overthink the day
like overthinking what
could have been
and rethinking what
never should have happened
overthinking what might be
and what I imagine should follow

here arrives a ladder-backed woodpecker
flitting to a fresh scar
glad I suppose for easy pickings

Songs

When the darkest of dark hours
spreads wings through the woods,
and storms bring darker clouds still,
when every sound, every crack and rustling
breaks the breathless silence
with pounding dread,

then there can be birds
aware of dawn arriving
before arrival, invisible
birds singing their heedless songs,
heedless of human needs
and feelings in simply announcing
a coming day come what may.

In time the choral warm-ups fade
to await their individual parts
giving way to solo prominence,
and there with varied repertoire
the wren sounds forth in loud providence
that brings a smile and calms the heart.

Then gates of despair open to the air,
as happens in nature's commune,
and as for me, if I could be,
I would be the wren.

Wall

from high up
    upper stories of the mind
green fields can be seen
stretching beyond the gray
    walled edge
    and beyond the green
north rising up mountains
    silver mists rising

and from high up
south way south
    beyond the sandy edge
oceans line their waves in rows
    from shades of deep green
to blue melting into distant sky

and from high up
eastern plains undulate
    golden sheaves of seeds
as if the future comes from there
as if freedom is only the new
    increase of light

and from high up
west way west
    cactus and mesquite
    spread rolling over hills
older than droughted sands
as if freedom will rest
    there where light sinks
        away

so there is still freedom

there beyond the gray wall
surrounding the ground floor
    of daily breathing
where sensations believe
    they are enough
of primal reasons

freedom still there beyond
        stretching away
            every way

not the mind that wouldn't
find a way beyond
        the gray edge
to freedom stretching away

not the heart that still sings
        songs of long ago
words of tenderness adrift
not the heart that promised
        what could not be kept
            that wouldn't
find a way beyond
        the gray edge
            stretching away

but faithless the corporeal
        breathes the enclosed
dust of obsessions
cowering in shades of fear
as if there were no music
        or poetry
that could lead the way
        away
            far away

to freedom
        there beyond
where lonely
        the unraveled soul
            awaits

Inevitably

inevitably the curtain falls
the last act done inevitably

we, the audience, have seen it all
what was it you said
and how we laughed with life
laughed and laughed
and how in anger and tragedy
we cried and found our empathy
how in the end you were afraid

inevitably we, the audience, know
the answer is still a mystery
not knowing what went before
there is no knowing after
after the curtain falls
what is behind on the silent stage

and we are left
silent with faith

inevitably there are tears
proving love like energy
is never lost
proving there is love
beyond the brief stage

and in passing decades
fresh tears prove once again
again and again
there is a timeless love
beyond absence
beyond the silence
we have always known
always feared

Where the Light Leads

Stepping into the heat
of the bare-boned night,
mortal truths are difficult,
freedom, fearful.

A foreign sound in the darkness
quickens the heart.

Midnight arrives lonely
waving impossible questions.
In that black sky faces
        are forgotten;
names, red-shifted abstractions;
memories, fairy tales
        in gilt frames.

Identity dissipates
like a winter breath,
            importance,
like smoke in a high wind.

Life recedes into the distant
        past,
futures dim to impossible
        glimmers.

Cold depths of space
        absorb beliefs
leaving pretenses
        adrift
like the dry air of sleep
        fitful
from desperate dreams.

So midnight becomes
        the yearning,
unfillable yearning
        for home,
for anything that fills.

Fear and emptiness summon
        violent fringes
flashing weapons like search
        lights cutting
the edge of the darkness,
pushing hope through narcotic
        syringes.

No amount of excess
        is enough
to sate the faithless
        heart.

The path is wide that relinquishes
        freedom
to follow deceitful leaders
who need no answers
        but rules,
no kinship but golden idols.

Where is the dawn
        to end the gloom?
Who knows words
        that might shine,
stories to fill the heart?

The stars have written nothing.
Their alignment follows
        larger designs,
darkness between them increases.

What had been foretold,
        myths to explain
the rise and fall
        of civilizations,
the long expected to come
        among us,
all that built community,
        now fade like echoes
down canyons of time.

Across the earth a great need
        has deepened.

The path intended
        toward safety
and fields spread
        wide and green
has entered desert sands.

Refugees homeless
in strange countries
        seek
some place far from tyrant
        commands,
from wanton leaders steeped
        in power and greed.

The net of life goes unmended,
        ends frayed
from the weight
        of commerce.

In silence sanctity is manifest.
In scarcity purity is manifest.
In presence mercy is manifest.
In reciprocity holiness is manifest.

Do not be afraid
for fear is irrelevant,
        worry, also, irrelevant.
Those who use fear as power
        are irrelevant.

Do not be afraid.
The myths are not gone,
        but recast.
The dance now staged
requires new rhythms,
        fresh steps.

Another story,
        another way
older than power,
older than civilization,
        another way
survives the imminence

of extinction.

The message arises
among the meek,
age to age, time after time,
whenever survival is at risk.

Ever present light
        shines from the eyes
of every creature,
shines from leaves,
        and jagged edges of stone.

Listen for songs
        that need singing,
as birds have sung their songs
        daily
through millions of years
        of catastrophes.

Do not follow the blindness
        of wealth.
Rather burn incense
for those who practice justice;
        give gold
to those who love
the precious beauty of living;
        give gifts
to honor those who show
compassion and sacrifice.

Where the light leads
over rolling hills
        there may yet be
a community rising up
        on the outskirts.

Sanctity

Words without sanctity
become the greatest sarcasm,
"forgive them knowing not"
just before the last spasms,
before the head hanging limply

suffering degradation from what
the madness of power does
because surely they do know
exactly what they do

when to take the advantage
with lies they pledge
        are true,
when to strike down
        with forceful blows,
when to proclaim divine rights,
when to pound
        fear into hands
and feet, pierce the side
with unreasoned guilt
        deftly planned,

how to bomb hospitals and schools,
press a knee
        to choke the neck,
how to build an economy for fools
that leaves them destitute
        in its wake.

In times of dominion,
unquestionable authority,
expectations overwhelm,
ignorance
        explodes.

Insidious as they are,
careless of suffering,
of futures beyond the cruelty
        of their lives,

of all they forsake,
thinking might
          is the way of life,

those words,
those unmistakable words,
"forgive them knowing not,"
are the sanctity needed
          in these times,

for draped in wasteful pleasures,
senseless from plastic ease,
          we are they.

Having unknowingly found
          powers of evolution
and achievements of unbelievable ease,
          we are they.

Having filled the earth
          with waste
not knowing consequences
          of profligacy

          we are they
who do not know the wages
          of greed,
          results of excess,
who do not know
how the burned particle
sets all the earth aflame.

We are they
with gun-barrel eyes
who do not know
how to establish justice
          or silence
the warring heart.

And I, one among the hosts,
I do not know
how intended good
          causes harm,

or how my simple comforts
        cause oppression
and pain across the world,
extinction of precious beings.

These, these are the times
in need of sanctity,
words that become
        kindness,
        deed by deed,
peace rising
        to fill every lung.

In the sanctity of those words,
"forgive them knowing not,"
vanity fades like morning mists
        burned away midday,
and pleasures that seemed the import
        of all,
pale within the humbled heart.

Esperanza

In the dry heat
buds appear clustered
that bloom bright as flame,
yellow trumpets
to announce beginnings,
trumpets to announce
endings.

Any who see the shine
in the green leaves
and the xanthous flowers
feel hope for the ages.

Inevitably weather brings
a freeze to the leaves
like news of war
to human minds,
like news of disease
and disaster
to human hearts.

The flowers drop
and leaves shrivel
as belief within the icy
tendrils of doubt.
The woody stems wither
and crack as assurance
within frigid gales
of cruelty and violence.

Brittle branches cut away,
by all accounts death has won.
Death, inevitably, always wins.

But from deep within roots
upon the increase of light,
like morning breaking
into a tomb,
slowly green leaves unfurl
from shoots.

And day by day
new life arises
soon to raise
a chorus of trumpets.

Requiem

softly softly clouds close
a furrowed brow
over the blueless sky

a slow shuffling of leaves
disturbs the empty silence

high above, a flock of wings
lift the last dance
high and away,
lifts
what had become of us
higher and higher away

whatever could have been
of us
now blends
into mists
that will not rise,
promises now lost
among wind-blown leaves

there are no stones
loud enough,
the wild has no howl
to overcome the hush

the epitaph
that might describe
us

cannot be seen,
is
only chiseled
deep
within the fading
heart
only escapes
in crumbles
in the moonless

dark

everything that could have been
has condensed
to dew
on angled leaves and limbs
droplets lined
like moments passing
that evanesce
into staggered breaths

the sun retreats
lost and wandering
elsewhere
to another day

clouds swallow the stars
one by one

darkness enshrouds
the world,
the universe

merciful phosphorescence,
living spark,
inspire assurance,

merciful phosphorescence,
eyes shining in the dark,
console presence

merciful phosphorescence,
memory of light,
resurrect peace.

Uprising

An impassioned uprising
I knew once, slope of hope
I knew like the palm of my hand,
has gone the way of thickets,
lost to me like the truth of legends.

You were there then
in the network of firing neurons
invisible yet present
across dark fields aware when
I leaned into the stars.

You remember don't you
the final genuflect of my leaving
off on my own without grieving
fearless in the face of stagnancy
taking my own doubtful way
as if mine would be the saving.

For so long I had hoped in my dreaming,
believed in the miracles of my believing.
I did not know how quickly
rime would coat my thinking,
how living could be the breaking
of all I had pledged in fantasy.

You were there, always there then
in the network of veins,
in my arterial pulse,
the folding of my brain,
always in my memory uprising
looking for the part of me
that never left.

Everywhere I have been
you have been the birdsong
before the morning breaking,
the thought before words forming,

yours, the air, same air

of a million dinosaurs breathing,
breath of every sentience,
breath of my own breathing.

Yours is the heart of my beating,
the song of my hearing;
mine, the ears of your singing,
the eyes of your seeing.

You are the entangled feelings
of uprising never leaving,
waiting without expectation.

meteor shower

flat against the supine roof
the sky spread its jeweled escape
over those ignorant youth
to a party come late

this was before thoughts of war
before the loss of truth
eyes unaccustomed to dark
when every flash was a muse

watching there among silent stars
moving in ancient red-shifting ways
watching for signs of who they are
those carefree youth watched amazed

for glimmering streaks however brief

to appear like silent streamers
at the end of fireworks displays
hoping wish upon wish for bright days

as only doe-eyed youth can believe

for them the world spins stars
not knowing they are memories
not sequins glittering
in a darkened mirror

and the light sent long before
there were myths to outline heroes
is a silent glimmering
as long long they fade

and the expected streamers
are just the dust left in the wake
of comets that passed by long ago

so each flash lasts but an instant

not pointing some future way
no matter what might be supposed
but like poems arrive from nowhere
on a clear night with reminiscent

messages burning the air

Elegy

Words, there should be words,
words, arrogant and vain
thinking they describe or explain,
thinking their meaning
might shape reality.

This should be a blank sheet
so white it disappears,
so black everything disappears
into it.

Colorful flowers?
why should there be flowers?
what do flowers have to do with absence?

Music? a hymn? Debussy or Satie?
expressions of sadness perhaps,
but sorrow?
how can music yield silence?

Oh there are words carved in stone,
sentiments that capture a lifetime
as much as a single lightning flash
captures a long storm.
And there are numbers carved,
a span, as if a clock tick
is the same as a galactic year.

No, there are no words
to evoke the hollow
in the sense realized
that certain things of true
meaning will never again be,
a particular smile remembered
and always looked for,
a particular gleam of sun

on hair, moonlight on a face,
the depths in certain eyes
that will never again be.

Oh music, wordless passion,
ceaseless echo in hollows,
there is a place in the heart
for music that begins a dirge,
a howl in dead of night
and whimpers into dawn
and settles finally into jazz
like background radiation,
the vibration that rings
beyond voiceless silence.

Oh flowers in the end
find their place rising
as from the latest mass extinction,
new to the world arising
wild and free in open fields,
spreading a blush of color
to a barren world,
foretelling in their brief
days of coming seeds
some time undefined
after shriveled petals
drop like tears.